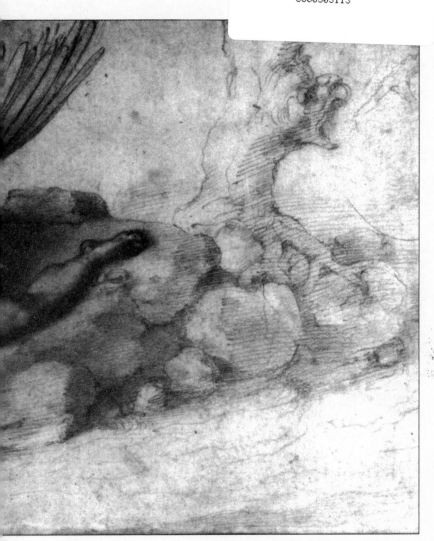

from Jean
Xmas 98.

Love Sonnets
and Madrigals to
Tommaso de'Cavalieri

Also translated by Michael Sullivan
The Idea of Prose by Giorgio Agamben

Love Sonnets and Madrigals to Tommaso de'Cavalieri

MICHELANGELO

*Translated from the Italian and with an
introduction by Michael Sullivan*

PETER OWEN
LONDON AND CHESTER SPRINGS

PETER OWEN PUBLISHERS
73 Kenway Road London SW5 0RE
Peter Owen books are distributed in the USA by
Dufour Editions Inc. Chester Springs PA 19425-0007

First published in Great Britain 1997
© Michael Sullivan 1997

ISBN 0 7206 1040 0

A catalogue record for this book is available from the British Library

Printed and made in Great Britain by Biddles of Guildford and King's Lynn

Illustrations appear courtesy of the Royal Collection © Her Majesty the Queen
Ganymede by Giulio Clovio after Michelangelo (title page; details on
pp. 44–5, 83); *Tityus* by Michelangelo (endpapers; details on pp. 20–21); *The
Fall of Phaeton* by Michelangelo (p. 17; details on pp. 34–5, 44, 45, 82, 102–3)

TO ERIC HEBBORN
persone belle e vive

Introduction

THE sonnets and madrigals to Tommaso de'Cavalieri have never been gathered as a group before. Together they constitute the largest sequence of poems composed by Michelangelo and the first large sequence of poems in any modern tongue – in this case the vernacular Florentine that, thanks to Dante, was to become the dominant strain in Italian – addressed by one man to another. There are three other subsidiary sequences of his poems; one, directed to the poet and mystic Vittoria Colonna, of about forty poems; a second, largely quatrains, consisting of epitaphs for the fifteen-year-old Cecchino Bracci produced at the insistence of Luigi del Ricchio, a literary collaborator of Michelangelo and uncle to the boy; and a third, the poems now considered a literary exercise, to 'la donna bella e crudele'.

Michelangelo had begun composing poetry some time before he was thirty in a desultory fashion, and little in his early production suggests that he would turn into the greatest lyric poet of his generation. What brought about the change was his meeting and love for Cavalieri. The intensity and complexity of feeling in their relationship brought out corresponding capacities to shape and deepen paradoxes of commitment, contradictory yearnings and opposing pressures that lasted into Michelangelo's old age. The period of their high exercise runs from 1532 to around 1548, the year after the death of Vittoria Colonna. From then on inspiration and production dwindled, though there are still some poems that encapsulate the power and skill that burst upon Michelangelo with his love for Cavalieri. It is the centrality of the experience that makes me describe

7

the other sequences as subsidiary, not any marked difference in formal skill or – the Bracci epitaphs apart – thematic interest. So unified was the impulse that dating and attribution of various poems to one cycle or the other has shifted backwards and forwards from editor to editor and translation to translation. This is less the result of Michelangelo's own shifts in the gender of possessives in his drafts, of his addressing Vittoria Colonna as 'signore', 'lord', or of the meddling appeasement practised in the first published edition by Michelangelo's great-nephew in his accommodation to the more perturbable society of 1623 but, rather, of a tautness of mind and pitch of feeling common to them all and occasioned by the inescapable beauty of Cavalieri.

Tommaso de'Cavalieri was born in Rome to Emiliano de'Cavalieri and a daughter of the Florentine banker Tommaso Bacelli. In the autumn or winter of 1532, when he was twenty-one or twenty-two, he was introduced to Michelangelo, then fifty-seven years old. The renowned sculptor, painter, architect agreed to do something he never had before done and was never to repeat again: he consented to give drawing lessons to his new friend. Later he was to do a drawing of Cavalieri, a full-length cartoon, something, as Vasari tells us, he refused to before and after because 'he abhorred drawing from life unless it was of infinite beauty'. Cavalieri's appearance at this time, his intellectual and moral gifts, were testified to in a public lecture given in Florence by Benedetto Varchi on Michelangelo's poetry, in particular on G. 98 and its mention of an 'armed cavalier': '. . . addressed to Tommaso Cavalieri, a most noble young Roman, in whom I recognised in Rome (apart from the incomparable beauty of his body) so much comeliness of behaviour, and such excellent wit and gracious manner, that he well deserved, and deserves still, to be the more loved by those who come to know him better'.

The first of Cavalieri's three letters to Michelangelo, dated 1 January 1533, speaks of his own artistic production, 'because of which you showed me no little affection'. Michelangelo's letters, in return, speak a great love. Donato Giannotti reports in his *Dialogi* (1546), a transcription of discussions on Dante held by Giannotti, Michelangelo, del Riccio and others, that Michelangelo declared himself 'of all men the most inclined to love persons', immediately adding that when he meets someone of great merit 'I am forced to fall in love with him'. The shift from the feminine plural of *persone* to the masculine singular, of particular help in the interpretation of the final line of sonnet G. 79, has large significance for the whole of Michelangelo's life. Whatever the full nature of the relationship with the man whom he described as 'light of our age, unique in the world', the friendship that followed was tenacious and enduring.

We know nothing of any sexual act of Michelangelo's, with man or woman, or even whether he engaged in any such. What evidence the love sonnets provide – a mention on 'loving arms' in G. 72 and the perverse imagery of G. 94 – is set in an optative, wishful tense, while the tenebrous guilt for 'great sin' of later poems remains generic. Whether, as Michelangelo claimed, his love for Cavalieri was chaste, their contemporaries thought otherwise, and the relationship caused much gossip and speculation. It was certainly, in an ample sense, erotic.

It began, as I have said, with drawing lessons. Cavalieri as pupil had sufficient talent to justify Michelangelo's enthusiasm and produced many drawings, most of them in 1533–4 at the time of the lessons. If they are now slighted it is not so much for their markedly non-professional execution as for the fact that they were earlier attributed to Michelangelo himself. This odd switching of their production was to happen again. Cavalieri's drawings, in fact, differ from Michelangelo's in their original style of composition and their psychological realism As we shall see, Michelangelo made considerable use of Cavalieri's capacities. The method of the lessons, it appears, was for Cavalieri to suggest a topic, make a drawing, and for Michelangelo, rather than correct it, to reply with a drawing on the same subject, which he then gave to Cavalieri. His gift of 'pictures' to Cavalieri is mentioned in sonnet G. 79.

These drawings, and others inherited from Sebastiano del Piombo, formed the basis of a collection that became famous in Cavalieri's lifetime. After his death the collection was bought by Alessandro Farnese for the remarkable sum of 500 scudi and most of it is now in Windsor Castle. *Tityus*, *The Fall of Phaeton* and *Ganymede* (now thought of as lost – Windsor has a copy by Giulio Clovio) were among those given directly to Cavalieri. Ludvig Goldscheider describes *Tityus* as Michelangelo's most erotic drawing after *Leda and the Swan*. The poor state of some of the drawings is the result of Cavalieri's generosity in lending them to copyists.

The drawing lessons continued after Michelangelo received the commission for the Sistine Chapel and Cavalieri produced a considerable number of sketches and studies for *The Last Judgement*. At least six of the figures in the finished fresco – including such important figures as St Lawrence, St Longinus and St Andrew – were taken up and developed by Michelangelo.

Though he enjoyed great consideration in Michelangelo's circle, with Sebastiano del Piombo, Leone Lioni, Daniele da

Volterra and Marcello Venusti, we know little more about him than that he was versatile – he also composed music – and intelligent, that in 1545 he married Lavinia della Valle, of the family of Cardinal Andrea della Valle, and that among his children was the musician Emilio, the Baroque composer, of great importance in the history of opera. Of his public life we know that his opinion was consulted by eminent men, he was appointed by Gregory XIII as adviser to Giacomo della Porta for the building of the Gregorian Chapel in the Vatican and commissioned two paintings of the Annunciation – one for St John Lateran and for S. Maria della Pace, from Venusti. In this way, and through his collection, it is likely he exercised considerable influence on the artistic notions of the artists and cognoscenti of his time.

Most of his adult life, the twenty-seven years between 1548 and 1575 when he resigned, was spent overseeing the construction of the buildings on the Capitoline Hill according to Michelangelo's designs. The façade of Palazzo dei Senatori on the Capitoline was for long attributed to Cavalieri himself and – the irony returns – for that reason slighted. Only recently has it been reattributed to Michelangelo, at whose deathbed in 1564, testimony to the tenacity of their relationship, Cavalieri was one of the four men present.

The full-length cartoon of 'Messer Tommaso' is lost. Yet we do have a clue to his great beauty. After seeing *The Last Judgement*, Aretino, a gossip and epigrammatist but also the confidant of many and in these things trustworthy, let it be known that Michelangelo had portrayed two of his lovers in the fresco and names one of them as Tommaso. It is the view of some Michelangelo scholars (Robert J. Clements, for example) that Cavalieri is portrayed in the principal figure, the Christus Judex.

There is not the space here for scholarly discussion of the publishing history of Michelangelo's poems, the influences on him and the mind-set of the age. In any case, the labour has already been performed, in English, by such people as Robert J. Clements, James M. Saslow and, most recently, Christopher Ryan. The Italian text on which I have based myself – as have all commentators and translators since 1960 – is that of the critical edition of Enzo Noè Girardi published in that year; hence the G. followed by his numbering which identifies the poems.

The picture that emerges from Michelangelo's own statements is that of a rhymer who took his own efforts to be rough and unprofessional; who sent his drafts to Luigi del Riccio and Donato Giannotti to be 'cobbled up'; who called his epitaphs for Cecchino Bracci *polizini*, vouchers, which, indeed, perhaps they were. Intended as only fifteen, the insistence of del Riccio and his encumbering gifts forced them to grow to a full forty-eight. The poet is the same man, however, who deprecated himself as a painter – a view no one has shared.

Indeed, many of the poems went through various drafts, though not necessarily to their improvement; and Christopher Ryan makes clear that Michelangelo was a more stringent formalist than the conventions of his age would have allowed. All autonomous quatrains, and all those of complete sonnets, rhyme ABBA. Of the sonnets given here, all except G. 98 and G. 101 have sestets that rhyme CDECDE. In the madrigal, always a much looser form, Michelangelo hardly ever has an unrhymed line-ending and never has more than two, though convention would have permitted three.

He also was concerned about their becoming public, sufficiently, on the one hand, to quarrel with del Riccio when some of the poems circulated without his permission and, on the other, to work with the same del Riccio towards a selection for publication, an enterprise that seems to have petered out with the untimely death of his collaborator.

As Italian poems Michelangelo's are startling, 'grammatically imperfect . . . contorted in expression and harsh in sound', says Ryan. It is common in – almost a commonplace of – criticism to compare the poems to the late sculptures: unfinished, still showing the chisel marks, dense with unresolved meaning, masterworks nevertheless. Sidney Alexander, with unusual aptness, compares Michelangelo to John Donne. If so, it is with the Donne who was seen as 'weav[ing] iron pokers into true love-knots' and who has to be construed 'according to the passion'. Of poets, Wordsworth found him 'the most difficult to construe that I have ever met with, but just what you would expect from such a man, showing abundantly how conversant his soul was with great things'.

My own view will seem too obvious. All that I want to do is point to the Italian word *rime*. Surely enough it is generic for poetry, but it insists upon a particular feature. Not metre, not scansion, nor even syntactical construction, but rhyme, is what Michelangelo is striving for. His concentration on this explains his extraordinary use of ellipsis, unusual word order, inversion, his packed lines, the lines padded merely to provide breathing space for the incisive rhyming word, his lack of care for syllable counting, even at times the sliding gender of his contents. I also think it is the reason why most of his translators have been poets and why a prose translation, however lucid, is bound to miss what is effortful in their intention and meaning, for, in some strong sense, these poems are created by their rhymes.

Two great poets, Wordsworth and Rilke, and various others – in English, Southey, John Addington Symonds, Longfellow, Emerson, Bridges, Elizabeth Jennings, Peter Porter – have translated some of Michelangelo's poems. The few who benefited, or might have benefited, from Girardi's work had too little Italian, took the original rightly or wrongly as impetus for poems of their own or, by smoothing and tuning to other rhyme schemes, have missed Michelangelo's scabrous pointedness. The translations that follow are a harrowed striving to remain faithful to his rhymes in the belief that more will follow. The notes indicate the related insufficiencies.

Had Eric Hebborn not died, this book would still have been dedicated to him. In Rome, in the spring of 1995, he showed me a drawing of Ganymede that he expected to be recognised as the lost *Ganymede*. It will be interesting to inspect its provenance should it ever reappear. At the same time he showed me his version of the Cavalieri cycle and asked my help, taking me to have better Italian and to know more of poetry. I made trial of a handful of poems. Neither of us was satisfied; Eric because they were too far removed from his version and me because they too far from the original. After his mysterious death I determined to carry through the project. I persuade myself he would be more satisfied now.

14

A note on the text

The aim of the notes at the end of the book is to clarify the deviance of the English version. They might be considered a catalogue of failure since they indicate the occasions on which my insistence on following Michelangelo's rhyme scheme has led me to shift the order of his lines or use enjambement where he does not. The uncertain orthography of his time allowed him, speaking of Cavalieri, to attach the singular possessive adjective *suo* to the feminine plural noun *bellezze*, beauties The startlement this may now cause should be held in check by the number of times in which he uses the current feminine plural *mie* of his own predicates, his eyes (masculine plural), his hairy skin (feminine singular). If it was, at times, an effect he meant, English cannot catch it. The reader should keep an eye on the Italian. Other syntactic liberties create fecund ambiguities and where I have spotted them but been unable to render them a note will tell. I leave unremarked the occasions where I have used a generic singular for his plural, or vice versa, as I do my inversions of such compilationary adjectives as 'rare' and 'unique'.

Michelangelo's imagery in these poems centres on the antitheses of light, dark, cold and heat. Many of the poems are sunlit, the more so since the genius of the Italian language allows him to contract *solo*, adjective and adverb, to *sol*, sun, an *en plus* irreproducible in English, though I do make one sole attempt. The word can occur as sunburst when Michelangelo is speaking of the singularity of de'Cavalieri and as false sunrise when he is speaking of his own solitariness. Both, and the sublunar dust above, can be glimpsed in the skyscape *en face*. 'I.t.o.': in the original, to which line numbers refer. Italics below indicate that a word or phrase occurs in the text, English or Italian.

15

Vivo della mia morte e, se ben guardo,
felice vivo d'infelice sorte;
e chi viver non sa d'angoscia e morte,
nel foco venga, ov'io mi struggo e ardo.

I live on death, and if rightly I discern
On my unhappy lot I live happy so,
Who cannot live on death and woe,
Enter this fire wherein I yearn and burn.

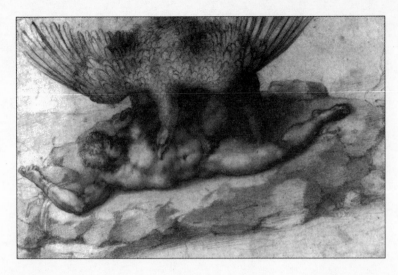

G 57

S'i' vivo più di chi più m'arde e cuoce,
quante più legne o vento il foco accende,
tanto più chi m'uccide mi difende,
e più mi giova dove più mi nuoce.

G 57

If I live most on what most burns and grills,
The more the fire may blaze with wind or wood,
The more the one who kills me does me good
And defends me most there where he does most ill.

Se l'immortal desio, c'alza e corregge
gli altrui pensier, traessi e' mie di fore,
forse c'ancor nella casa d'Amore
farie pietoso chi spietato regge.

Ma perché l'alma per divina legge
ha lunga vita, e 'l corpo in breve muore,
non può 'l senso suo lode o suo valore
appien descriver quel c'appien non legge.

Dunche, oilmè! come sarà udita
la casta voglia che 'l cor dentro incende
da chi sempre se stesso in altrui vede?

La mia giornata m'è impedita
col mie signor c'alle menzogne attende,
c'a dire il ver, bugiardo è chi nol crede.

Were the immortal urge that right and rise
Men's thoughts, now to bring mine to light
He who ruthless rules Love's house might
On me yet again in pity turn his eyes.
But since in brief time the body dies
While the soul lives long by divine right,
Its praise or worth carnal sense does slight
In describing what it scarce descries.
And so, poor me! what hearing now will get
The chaste desire that in my bosom burns
From those who others as themselves will judge?
My happy time with him has suffered let
For my dearest lord to false rumour turns,
To tell the truth, they lie who credence grudge.

S'un casto amor, s'una pietà superna,
s'una fortuna infra due amanti equale,
s'un'aspra sorte all'un dell'altro cale,
s'un spirto, s'un voler duo cor governa;

    s'un'anima in duo corpi è fatta etterna,
ambo levando al cielo e con pari ale;
s'Amor d'un colpo e d'un dorato strale
le viscer di duo petti arda e discerna;

    s'aman l'un l'altro e nessun se medesmo,
d'un gusto e d'un diletto, a tal mercede
c'a un fin voglia l'uno l'altro porre:

    se mille e mille, non sarien centesmo
a tal nodo d'amore, a tanta fede;
e sol l'isdegno il può rompere e sciorre.

If a chaste love, if a lofty piety uphold,
If but one fortune should two lovers share,
If one in bitter case the other care,
If one wish, one spirit two hearts enfold;
If two bodies make one immortal soul,
Raising both to heaven on wings matched fair;
If the innards of two breasts Love burn and tear
With but one single shot, one shaft of gold;
If each the other love and not himself apart,
With relish and delight to such degree
Each for the other impose a single lot;
Thousand thousand ifs were no hundredth part
Of such a bond of love, of so much loyalty;
And disdain alone can break it and unknot.

Tu sa' ch'i' so, signor mie, che tu sai
ch'i' vengo per goderti più da presso,
e sai ch'i' so che tu sa' ch'i' son desso:
a che più indugio a salutarci omai?

Se vera è la speranza che mi dai,
se vero è 'l gran desio che m'è concesso,
rompasi il mur fra l'uno e l'altra messo,
ché doppia forza hann' i celati guai.

S'i' amo sol di te, signor mie caro,
quel che di te più ami, non ti sdegni,
ché l'un dell'altro spirto s'innamora.

Quel che nel tuo bel volto bramo e 'mparo
e mal compres' è dagli umani ingegni,
chi 'l vuol saper convien che prima mora.

You know I know, my lord, that you do know
I've come here to enjoy and breathe your air,
And know I know you know that I'm aware:
What reason, then, put off our meeting so?
If that hope is true which in me you grow,
If the great desire allowed is true as rare,
Break down the wall that stands between us there,
Since sorrows are doubled that hidden go.
If, my beloved lord, I only love in you
That which you love best, do not scorn,
Both enamoured be of the other's spirit.
For what in your fair face I learn and sue
And is misjudged by the human born,
It wants death to make understanding fit.

S'i' avessi creduto al primo sguardo
di quest'alma fenice al caldo sole
rinnovarmi per foco, come suole
nell'ultima vecchiezza, ond'io tutt'ardo,
    qual più veloce cervio o lince o pardo
segue 'l suo bene e fugge quel che dole,
agli atti, al riso, all'oneste parole
sarie cors'anzi, ond'or son presto e tardo.
    Ma perché più dolermi, po' ch'i' veggio
negli ochi di quest'angel lieto e solo
mie pace, mie riposo e mie salute?
    Forse che prima sarie stato il peggio
vederlo, udirlo, s'or di pari a volo
seco m'impenna a seguir suo virtute.

Had I believed when I first caught sight
Of this loved phoenix for whom I am on fire
That in its warm sun, and through the pyre,
As it in late age renews, that so I might,
Then like the stag or lynx or pard in flight
From what gives pain or chasing its desire,
I would have early run – am eager now, but tire –
To catch his every act, his smile, his upright
Words. But why do I complain, have I not seen
In his gladding unique angel's eye
My peace, my rest, my soul's immortal need?
Early to see him, hear him, worse had been
Since now on equal wing with him I fly
Soaring aloft to where his virtue lead.

Sol pur col foco il fabbro il ferro stende
al concetto suo caro e bel lavoro,
ne senza foco alcuno artista l'oro
al sommo grado suo raffina e rende;
    né l'unica fenice sé riprende
se non prim'arsa, ond'io s'ardendo moro,
spero più chiar resurger tra coloro
che morte accresce e 'l tempo non offende.
    Del foco, di ch'i' parlo, ho gran ventura
c'ancor per rinnovarmi abbi in me loco,
sendo già quasi nel numer de' morti.
    O ver, s'al cielo ascende per natura,
al suo elemento, e ch'io converso in foco
sie, come fie che seco non mi porti?

With fire alone can smiths make flattened
Iron for the fine work that they conceive,
Nor except through flame can art achieve
In gold the high purity the fire does rend;
Nor can the rare phoenix itself amend
Less it has burned before; hence do I believe
That if I burning die new life I shall receive
With those whom death exalts nor time offends.
The fire I speak of, for my luck is high,
Can yet to renew my life find range,
Though now I count myself as all but dead.
But since to heaven its nature is to fly
To join its element, and I to fire do change,
How may it be that with it I'm not sped?

Sì amico al freddo sasso è 'l foco interno
che, di quel tratto, se lo circumscrive,
che l'arda e spezzi, in qualche modo vive,
legando con sé gli altri in loco etterno.

E se 'n fornace dura, istate e verno
vince, e 'n più pregio che prima s'ascrive,
come purgata infra l'altre alte e dive
alma nel ciel tornasse da l'inferno.

Così tratto di me, se mi dissolve
arso e po' spento aver più vita posso.

Dunche, s'i' vivo, fatto fumo e polve,
etterno ben sarò, s'indurro al foco;
da tale oro e non ferro son percosso.

Such friend the cold stone finds in inner fire
That when drawn out it wraps it in a flame
That burns and breaks and yet it lives the same,
And binds others with it in place everlasting.
And if it face the furnace then it can tame
Summer and winter, the more merit earning,
Like a soul among the blessed and high returning
When hell has purged it thoroughly of blame.
In the same fashion, if be dissolved I must
By the hidden fire that plies within me,
Burned, then slack, I'll have life manifold.
Thus, if I live, though made of smoke and dust,
Tempered by flame, I'll joy eternally:
It was not iron to strike me so but gold.

Se 'l foco il sasso rompe e 'l ferro squaglia,
figlio del lor medesimo e duro interno,
che farà 'l più ardente dell'inferno
d'un nimico covon secco di paglia?

G 64

If fire splits stone and makes the iron flow,
Though child of their own resistant core,
What will hell do, which burns the more,
To a dried-out stook of straw its foe?

In quel medesmo tempo ch'io v'adoro,
la memoria del mie stato infelice
nel pensier mi ritorna, e piange e dice:
ben ama chi ben arde, ov'io dimoro.
Però che scudo fo di tutti loro . . .

G 65

In the very instant that I worship you,
The memory of my unhappy days
comes to mind and weeping says:
Who burns well loves well, which I do.
Though how of all this I shield construe . . .

Se nel volto per gli occhi il cor si vede,
altro segno non ho più manifesto
della mie fiamma; addunche basti or questo,
signor mie caro, a domandar mercede.

Forse lo spirto tuo, con maggior fede
ch'i' non credo, che sguarda il foco onesto
che m'arde, fie di me pietoso e presto,
come grazia c'abbonda a chi ben chiede.

O felice quel dì, se questo è certo!
Fermisi in un momento il tempo e l'ore,
il giorno e 'l sol nella su' antica traccia;

acciò ch'i' abbi, e non già per mie merto,
il desïato mie dolce signore
per sempre nell'indegne e pronte braccia.

If through the eyes the heart one reads
Then I own no clearer sign than these
Of my flame; therefore let it please,
dear lord, that they demand my meed.
With greater trust than I can creed,
Your spirit, when the honest fire it sees
As burns in me, may pity me and ease,
For grace abounds to him who rightly pleads.
O happy that day, for surely it's true!
Let time and the hours stop on the word,
The sun in his ancient round, the day;
That I may have, and not by my due,
My most desired, my gracious lord
In my unworthy but ready arms always.

Mentre del foco son scacciata e priva,
morir m'è forza, ove si vive e campa;
e 'l mie cibo è sol quel c'arde e avvampa
e di quel c'altri muor, convien ch'i' viva.

When I'm deprived and driven from the flame,
Perforce I die where people live and thrive;
On what burns and flares alone I feed to keep alive,
Though death to others, I flourish on the same.

I' piango, i' ardo, i' mi consumo, e 'l core
di questo si nutrisce. O dolce sorte!
chi è che viva sol della suo morte,
come fo io d'affanni e di dolore?
    Ahi! crudel arcier, tu sai ben l'ore
da far tranquille l'angosciose e corte
miserie nostre con la tuo man forte;
ché chi vive di morte mai non muore.

I am aflame, consume myself, and cry;
On this, O sweetest fate! my heart is fed,
Who is there lives alone on death not dead
And on travail and on his pain as I?
Ah! cruel archer, how well you spy
The hour to bate our misery anguishèd
And short with your hand dread;
So he who lives on death does never die.

G 75

Egli è pur troppo a rimirarsi intorno
chi con la vista ancide i circustanti
sol per mostrarsi andar diporto attorno.
    Egli è pur troppo a chì fa notte il giorno,
scurando il sol co' vaghi e be' sembianti,
aprirgli spesso, e chi con risi e canti
ammuta altrui non esser meno adorno.

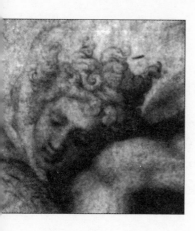

G 75

Too much he is, glancing this way that way,
When the sight kills those standing there,
Just showing himself on strolling holiday.
Too much, that he who turns the bright day
Night, dimming the sun with eyes so fair,
Open them oft, that who with smiles and air
Dumbs others, should have no less array.

Non so se s'è la desïata luce
del suo primo fattor, che l'alma sente,
o se della memoria della gente
alcun'altra beltà nel cor traluce;
    o se fama o se sogno alcun produce
agli occhi manifesto, al cor presente,
di sé lasciando un non so che cocente
ch'è forse or quel c'a pianger mi conduce.
    Quel ch'i' sento e ch'i' cerco e chi mi guidi
meco non è; né so ben veder dove
trovar mel possa, e par c'altri mel mostri.
    Questo, signor, m'avvien, po' ch'i' vi vidi,
c'un dolce amaro, un sì e no mi muove:
certo saranno stati gli occhi vostri.

I do not know if it is the wanted light
Of its first maker which the soul sense,
Or if out of mankind's remembrance
In the heart another beauty's bright;
Or if renown or if dream give sight
To eyes plain, to the heart a presence,
That leaves its own scalding essence
So that weep even now I might.
What I feel, what seek, who might guide
With me is not; nor for myself where to look
Know not, though others seem to show.
This, since I first saw you, my lord, abides,
There's a bitter sweet, by yes and no I'm shook:
Your eyes they will have been I owe.

Se 'l foco fusse alla bellezza equale
degli occhi vostri, che da que' si parte,
non avrie 'l mondo si gelata parte
che non ardessi com'acceso strale.

Ma 'l ciel, pietoso d'ogni nostro male,
a noi d'ogni beltà, che 'n voi comparte,
la visiva virtù toglie e diparte
per tranquillar la vita aspr'e mortale.

Non è par dunche il foco alla beltate,
ché sol di quel' s'infiamma e s'innamora
altri del bel del ciel, ch'è da lui inteso.

Così n'avvien, signore, in questa etate:
se non vi par per voi ch'i' arda e mora,
poca capacità m'ha poco acceso.

If fire and beauty in equal parts
Were out of your eyes to flare
Earth had no zone so frozen bare
As not to blaze like a flaming dart.
Yet heaven, piteous of our smarts,
Of their striking power takes care
To rid all the beauties you share,
So softening this bitter life and short.
Thus fire is not up to beauty's gauge,
For it only loves, is fired, by what
Of heaven's beauty that gives sight.
So happens, my lord, at my age;
If it seem I burn not for you, die not,
Being little able I'm little set alight.

Dal dolce pianto al doloroso riso,
da una etterna e una corta pace
caduto son: là dove 'l ver si tace
soprasta 'l senso a quel da lui diviso.

Né so se dal mie core o dal tuo viso
la colpa vien del mal, che men dispiace
quante più cresce, o dall'ardente face
de gli occhi tuo rubati al paradiso.

La tuo beltà non è cosa mortale,
ma fatta su dal ciel fra noi divina;
ond'io perdendo ardendo mi conforto,

c'appresso a te non esser posso tale.
Se l'arme il ciel del mie morir destina,
chi può, s'i' muoio, dir c'abbiate il torto?

From sweet tears to smiles of bitter gall
From eternal peace to one so short
Am fallen: where truth's to silence brought
Those split from it are in the senses' thrall.
Nor for this pain, that less does pall
The more it grow, know if my heart to sort
Or your face, your eyes whose glowing wrought
From out of paradise was stolen all.
Your beauty is not a mortal thing,
But made on high divine for us below;
Hence though I lose, in burning I find balm,
For near you naught else is my being.
If for my dying heaven should bestow,
Who, if I die, can blame you for the arms?

Felice spirto, che con zelo ardente,
vecchio alla morte, in vita il mio cor tieni,
e fra mill'altri tuo diletti e beni
me sol saluti fra più nobil gente;
    come mi fusti agli occhi, or alla mente,
per l'altru' fiate a consolar mi vieni,
onde la speme il duol par che raffreni,
che non men che 'l disio l'anima sente.
    Dunche, trovando in te chi per me parla
grazia di te per me fra tante cure,
tal grazia ne ringrazia chi ti scrive.
    Che sconcia e grande usur saria a farla,
donandoti turpissime pitture
per riaver persone belle e vive.

Blithe spirit who with ardent zeal
My heart, old to death, keeps awake,
Greets me mid men of nobler make
Mid your thousand other joys and weal.
As then my eyes, now my mind you heal,
Come to console, the place of others take,
So hope, it seems, reins in that ache
The soul no less than desire now feels.
So finding in you one who speaks for me
Grace from you mid your many chores,
The writer's thanks for such benevolence.
How tawdry it would be and great usury
To give you pictures so piteous poor
To get return of fine and living presence.

I' mi credetti, il primo giorno ch'io
mira' tante bellezze uniche e sole,
fermar gli occhi com'aquila nel sole
nella minor di tante ch'i' desio.
Po' conosciut'ho il fallo e l'erro mio:
ché chi senz'ale un angel seguir volle,
il seme a' sassi, al vento le parole
indarno isparge, e l'intelletto a Dio.
Dunche, s'appresso il cor non mi sopporta
l'infinita beltà che gli occhi abbaglia,
né di lontan par m'assicuri o fidi,
      che fie di me? qual guida o quale scorta
fie che con teco ma' mi giovi o vaglia,
s'appresso m'ardi e nel partir m'uccidi?

I did believe myself on that first day
I saw such beauty rare and sole in kind,
Like an eagle in the sun made blind
By the least I desire of that array.
Later I found where my error lay:
Who'd follow an angel from behind
Wingless probe God with his mind,
Seed on stone, word on the wind casts away.
If, when near, my heart cannot support
The boundless beauty that dazzles my eye,
Nor, when at remove, comfort me and still,
What shall I do? what guide or escort
Will ever help and ward when you are by,
If close you burn and as you leave you kill?

Ogni cosa ch'i' veggio mi consiglia
e priega e forza ch'i' vi segua e ami;
ché quel che non è voi non è 'l mie bene.
Amor, che sprezza ogni altra maraviglia,
per mie salute vuol ch'i' cerchi e brami
voi, sole, solo; e così l'alma tiene
d'ogni alta spene e d'ogni valor priva;
e vuol ch'i' arda e viva
non sol di voi, ma di chi voi somiglia
degli occhi e delle ciglia alcuna parte.
E chi da voi si parte,
occhi, mie vita, non ha luce poi;
chè 'l ciel non è dove non siate voi.

Everything I behold now counsels me,
Pleads and urges that I love you and pursue;
For that which is not you is not my good.
Love, which mocks all other prodigy,
Decrees my welfare is to yearn and seek you,
My sole sun; and the spirit would
Of all high hope, all value, so deprive;
Decrees I burn, remain alive
Not just by you but even by he
Whose eyes or lashes are like in any way.
And who should from you stray,
Eyes, my life, light shall have none then:
For where you are not there is no heaven.

Non posso altra figura immaginarmi
o di nud'ombra o di terrestre spoglia,
col più alto pensier, tal che mie voglia
contra la tua beltà di quella s'armi.

Ché da te mosso, tanto scender parmi,
c'Amor d'ogni valor mi priva e spoglia,
ond'a pensar di minuir mie doglia
duplicando, la morte vien a darmi.

Però non val che più sproni mie fuga,
doppiando 'l corso alla beltà nemica,
ché 'l men dal più veloce non si scosta.

Amor con le sue man gli occhi m'asciuga,
promettendomi cara ogni fatica;
ché vile non può chi tanto costa.

I can conceive no other image
Either stark shade or empty flesh
In loftiest thought such that my wish
Against your beauty might battle wage
Away from you I go so deep I gauge,
That Love in me does all worth abolish
Wherefore by my rusing to diminish
Pain with doubling death does me contage.
So, futile to further spur and fly,
Matching my rival beauty's speed,
The less from the faster never draws away.
With his own hand Love dries my eye,
Promising each toil shall have its meed;
Base cannot be what asks so much to pay.

Veggio nel tuo bel viso, signor mio,
quel che narrar mal puossi in questa vita:
l'anima, della carne ancora vestita,
con esso è già più volte ascesa a Dio.

E se 'l vulgo malvagio, isciocco e rio,
di quel che sente, altrui segna e addita,
non è l'intensa voglia men gradita,
l'amor, la fede e l'onesto desio.

A quel pietoso fonte, onde siàn tutti,
s'assembra ogni beltà che qua si vede
più c'altra cosa alle persone accorte;

né altro saggio abbiàn né altri frutti
del cielo in terra; e chi v'ama con fede
trascende a Dio e fa dolce la morte.

In your fair face, my lord, I own
What can in life be scarcely told:
My soul still it in its fleshly mould
Often by means of it to God has flown
If the evil mob, stupid, quarrel-prone,
Points finger at others for what itself holds,
The intense wish is welcome as of old,
The love, trust, the desire true grown.
All beauty here seen, in its kind suits,
More than aught else, for who sees just,
The fount whence all come, the mercy seat;
Nor other taste have we, nor other fruits
Of heaven on earth; who loves you with trust
Transcends to God and makes death sweet.

Sì come nella penna e nell'inchiostro
è l'alto e 'l basso e 'l mediocre stile,
e ne' marmi l'immagin ricca e vile,
secondo che 'l sa trar l'ingegno nostro;

così, signor mie car, nel petto vostro,
quante l'orgoglio è forse ogni atto umile;
ma io sol quel c'a me propio è e simile
ne traggo, come fuor nel viso mostro.

Chi semina sospir, lacrime e doglie,
(l'umor dal ciel terrestre, schietto e solo,
a vari semi vario si converte),

però pianto e dolor ne miete e coglie;
chi mira alta beltà con sì gran duolo,
ne ritra' doglie e pene acerbe e certe.

Just as in the ink and in the pen
Is the high, the low and middling style,
And in marble the rich image and the vile
According to what our wits can ken;
In your breast, dear lord, there's then
Pride perhaps as much as humble trial;
But only what's fit and like to me I'll
Take, as in my face shows open.
Who sows sighs, tears and pains
(the pure clear humour from the sky
For the various seeds various turns)
Thus weeping and woe reaps and gains;
Who aims in torment at beauty high
Bitter and certain pangs he earns.

Vorrei voler, Signor, quel ch'io non voglio:
tra 'l foco e 'l cor di ghiaccia un vel s'asconde
che 'l foco ammorza, onde non corrisponde
la penna all'opre, e fa bugiardo 'l foglio.
I' t'amo con la lingua, e poi mi doglio
c'amor non giunge al cor; né so ben onde
apra l'uscio alla grazia che s'infonde
nel cor, che scacci ogni spietato orgoglio.
Squarcia 'l vel tu, Signor, rompi quel muro
che con la suo durezza ne ritarda
il sol della tuo luce, al mondo spenta!
Manda 'l preditto lume a noi venturo,
alla tuo bella sposa, acciò ch'io arda
il cor senz'alcun dubbio, e te sol senta.

Would I wanted, Lord, what I don't desire:
Between fire and heart a veil of ice to go
That damps the heat, makes the pen foe
To the work and turns the page a liar.
I love you with my tongue, then dire
Complain love reach not the heart; nor know
Where the gate opens that grace might flow
Therein and make pitiless pride retire.
Tear you the veil, Lord, break down the wall
Which in its hardness now holds back
The sun of your light, darkened to the whole!
Send the destined light promised to us all,
To your fair bride, so that all doubt lack
And only you I feel as I burn in soul.

Sento d'un foco un freddo aspetto acceso
che lontan m'arde e sé con seco agghiaccia;
pruovo una forza in due leggiadre braccia
che muove senza moto ogni altro peso.
    Unico spirto e da me solo inteso,
che non ha morte e morte altrui procaccia,
veggio e truovo chi, sciolto, 'l cor m'allaccia,
e da chi giova sol mi sento offeso.
    Com'esser può, signor, che d'un bel volto
ne porti 'l mio così contrari effetti,
se mal può chi non gli ha donar altrui?
    Onde al mio viver lieto, che m'ha tolto,
fa forse come 'l sol, se nol permetti,
che scalda 'l mondo e non è caldo lui.

I feel as lit by fire a cold countenance
That burns me from afar and keeps itself ice-chill;
A strength I feel two shapely arms to fill
Which without motion moves every balance.
Unique spirit and my minds sole tendance,
Who is undying yet others seeks to kill,
I find one binds my heart, unbound his will,
And for who gladdens only I feel grievance.
How can it be, lord, that a face so lovely
Should work on mine in contrary fashion,
For who has no ill can hardly others harm?
To the glad life that's taken from me,
It behaves, save you forbid it, like the sun,
It heats the world and yet itself's not warm.

Veggio co' be' vostr'occhi un dolce lume
che co' mie ciechi già veder non posso;
porto co' vostri piedi un pondo addosso,
che de' mie zoppi non è già costume .

Volo con le vostr'ale senza piume;
col vostro ingegno al ciel sempre son mosso;
dal vostro arbitrio son pallido e rosso,
freddo al sol, caldo alle più fredde brume.

Nel voler vostro è sol la voglia mia,
i miei pensier nel vostro cor si fanno,
nel vostro fiato son le mie parole.

Come luna da sé sol par ch'io sia,
ché gli occhi nostri in ciel veder non sanno
se non quel tanto che n'accende il sole.

G 89

I see a tender light through your fair eye
That my dim ones already cannot see;
I bear with your feet a weight upon me,
My lame ones now lack skill to try.
Plumeless with your wings I fly;
Rise by your wit to the apogee;
Am pale or redden by your decree
Cold in the sun, in the coldest fogs I fry.
In your wish alone are my wishes born,
In your breath my words are new,
My thoughts are made in your heart.
It seems I'm like the moon forlorn,
Which our eyes in heaven cannot view
Save that the sun should kindle part.

I' mi son caro assai più ch'i' non soglio;
poi ch'i' t'ebbi nel cor più di me vaglio,
come pietra c'aggiuntovi l'intaglio
è di più pregio che 'l suo primo scoglio.
O come scritta o pinta carta o foglio
più si riguarda d'ogni straccio o taglio,
tal di me fo, da po' ch'i' fu' berzaglio
segnato dal tuo viso, e non mi doglio.
Sicur con tale stampa in ogni loco
vo, come quel c'ha incanti o arme seco,
c'ogni periglio gli fan venir meno.
I' vaglio contr'a l'acqua e contr'al foco,
col segno tuo rallumino ogni cieco,
e col mie sputo sano ogni veleno.

I'm much dearer to me than is my bent;
With you in my heart I'm more than net,
Like stone that's been with cutting fret
Means more than the crude rock meant.
And less regard is paid to scrap or oddment
Than paper or page with words or painting set,
Such my vaunt since being the target
Stricken by your face, and I don't lament.
Every place I go your mark is guard,
Safe as one with arms or talisman,
Whereby all perils are made vain.
Against water, against fire, I am ward,
By your seal I give light to the blindman,
And with my spittle heal every bane.

Perc'all'estremo ardore
che toglie e rende poi
il chiuder e l'aprir degli occhi tuoi
duri più la mie vita,
fatti son calamita
di me, de l'alma e d'ogni mie valore;
tal c'anciderm' Amore,
forse perch'è pur cieco,
indugia, triema e teme.
C'a passarmi nel core,
sendo nel tuo con teco,
pungere' prima le tuo parte streme;
e perché meco insieme
non more, non m'ancide. O gran martire,
c'una doglia mortal, senza morire,
raddoppia quel languire
del qual, s'l' fussi meco, sare' fora.
Deh rendim' a me stesso, acciò ch'i' mora.

That to the intensest heat
The close and opening of your eyes
Takes away then reapplies
My life may longer last
They are become magnets fast
For me, my soul, my powers complete;
So though death he would mete,
Because he's blind alas,
Love lingers, shakes, forfends.
If mine within yours beat,
Through my heart to pass,
He must first your outside rend;
And lest with me you end,
Me he does not slay. O suffering,
For a mortal pain, with no dying,
Doubles the pining
Which would, were I my own, pass by.
Oh give me back myself that I may die.

Quantunche 'l tempo ne costringa e sproni
ognor con maggior guerra
a rendere alla terra
le membra afflitte, stanche e pellegrine,
non ha però 'ncor fine
chi l'alma attrista e me fa così lieto.
Né par che men perdoni
a chi 'l cor m'apre e serra,
nell'ore più vicine
e più dubbiose d'altro viver quieto;
ché l'error consueto,
com più m'attempo, ognor più si fa forte.
O dura mia più c'altra crudel sorte!
Tardi orama' puo' tormi tanti affanni;
c'un cor che arde e arso già molt'anni
torna, se ben l'ammorza la ragione,
non più già cor, ma cenere e carbone.

Though times presses and prods me on
Each hour with greater fray
To give back to the clay
My tired worn limbs and sore
But he will yet do more
Who saddens my soul yet so glad makes.
Nor does it seem he'll pardon
– he who unlocks my heart or bars the way –
In the hours just before
And most doubtful if to peace I'll reawake;
That the usual mistake,
The older I grow gets ever worse.
O harsher is mine than any cruel curse!
To lighten my burdens it's late for you;
A heart that burns, for years burnt through,
Turns, should reason slack the whole,
Not heart again but ash and charcoal.

G 93

Spargendo il senso il troppo ardor cocente
fuor del tuo bello, in alcun altro volto,
men forza ha, signor, molto
qual per più rami alpestro e fier torrente.
Il cor, che del più ardente
foco più vive, mal s'accorda allora
co' rari pianti e men caldi sospiri.
L'alma all'error presente
gode c'un di lor mora
per gire al ciel, là dove par c'aspiri.
La ragione i martiri
fra lor comparte; e fra più salde tempre
s'accordan tutt'a quattro amarti sempre.

Spreading its scorching beams
From your beauty to some other face,
Sense, my lord, will have less pace
As branches split a fiece Alpine stream.
The Heart, the hotter the fire should seem
Is more alive, so can't agree
With rare tears and sighs of cooler strain.
Alert to the mistaken theme
The Soul's glad one should cease
So as to go to heaven where it aims.
Reason divides the pains
Between; and with firmer sinew
All four agree to always loving you.

D'altrui pietoso e sol di sé spietato
nasce un vil bruto, che con pena e doglia
l'altrui man veste e la suo scorza spoglia
e sol per morte si può dir ben nato.

Così volesse al mie signor mie fato
vestir suo viva di mie morta spoglia,
che, come serpe al sasso si discoglia,
pur per morte potria cangiar mie stato.

O fussi sol la mie l'irsuta pelle
che, del suo pel contesta, fa tal gonna
che con ventura stringe sì bel seno,

ch'i' l'are' pure il giorno; o le pianelle
che fanno a quel di lor basa e colonna,
ch'i' pur ne porterei duo nevi almeno.

Piteous of others and to its sole self fell
A grubby beast is born, in grief and dread
Garbs others' hands, its outside peels instead
And only in its death can one say born well.
So would my lord my fate did tell
I'd dress his living body with mine dead
So, like a snake on the stone does shed
I'd better my life through my knell.
Oh if only it were my hirsute skin
With his hair wove made up the garment
Has the luck to clasp his splendid torso,
By day I'd have him too; or the bootikins
Which serve as his pillar and pediment,
Then I'd carry him two winters or more so.

Rendete agli occhi miei, o fonte o fiume,
l'onde della non vostra e salda vena,
che più v'innalza e cresce, e con più lena
che non è 'l vostro natural costume.

E tu, folt'aïr, ch 'l celeste lume
tempri a' trist'occhi, de' sospir mie piena,
rendigli al cor mie lasso e rasserena
tua scura faccia al mie visivo acume.

Renda la terra i passi alle mie piante,
c'ancor l'erba germugli che gli è tolta,
e 'l suono eco, già sorda a' mie lamenti;

gli sguardi agli occhi mie tuo luce sante,
ch'i' possa altra bellezza un'altra volta
amar, po' che di me non ti contenti.

O fountain O river give back to my eyes
The wave of that steady spate not yours,
Which rises and swells you with a force
That does not within your natural habit lie.
And you dense air full of my sighs ,
The sun for sad eyes makes less coarse,
Yield them and give my worn heart pause
Your dark face softening to my eyes.
Let the earth return the steps to my feet,
That the grass may sprout again they wore,
And Echo, deaf to my lament, the sound;
My glances from your blessed eyes retreat
That another beauty I may love once more
Since now by you I am too little found.

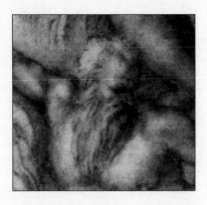

G 96

Si come secco legno in foco ardente
arder poss'io, s'i' non t'amo di core,
e l'alma perder, se null'altro sente.
    E se d'altra beltà spirto d'amore
fuor de' tu' occhi è che m'infiammi o scaldi,
tolti sien quegli a chi sanz'essi muore.
    S'io non t'amo e ador, ch'e' mie più baldi
pensier sien con la speme tanto tristi
quanto nel tuo amor fermi e saldi.

G 96

Like dry wood in the fire's blaze
If I love not with the heart let me burn out,
And lose my soul if it feel other ways.
If love kindles and makes me burn about
Anything other than your eyes' beauty,
Take them away, though I die without,
If I do not love you and am not aflame, be
My boldest thoughts with hope as dull
As now in your love they are firm and steady.

Al cor di zolfo, a la carne di stoppa,
a l'ossa che di secco legno sièno;
a l'alma senza guida e senza freno
al desir pronto, a la vaghezza troppa;
  a la cieca ragion debile e zoppa
al vischio, a' lacci di che 'l mondo è pieno;
non è gran maraviglia, in un baleno
arder nel primo foco che s'intoppa.

A la bell'arte che, se dal ciel seco
ciascun la porta, vince la natura,
quantunche sé ben prema in ogni loco;
  s'i' nacqui a quella né sordo né cieco,
proporzionato a che 'l cor m'arde e fura,
colpa è di chi m'ha destinato al foco.

With a heart of sulphur, with flesh of tow,
Instead of bones dry wood there;
With a soul unsteered, for pause no care
To desire prompt, to beauty over so;
With reason blind, weak and slow
To the birdlime, the traps everywhere;
It is no great marvel if in one flare
I burn in the first fire I stumbling go.
To that fair art each brings behind
From heaven to drive nature back,
Though still on all it stamps its name;
Since to that I was born nor deaf nor blind,
To the degree that he burns my heart and racks,
The fault is his who fated me to flame.

A che più debb'i' omai l'intensa voglia
sfogar con pianti o con parole meste,
se di tal sorte 'l ciel, che l'alma veste,
tard' o per tempo alcun mai non ne spoglia?
A che 'l cor lass' a più languir m'invoglia,
s'altri pur dee morir? Dunche per queste
luci l'ore del fin fian men moleste;
c'ogni altro ben val men c'ogni mia doglia.
Però se 'l colpo ch'io ne rub' e 'nvolo
schifar non posso, almen, s'è destinato,
chi entrerà 'nfra la dolcezza e 'l duolo?
Se vint' e preso i' debb'esser beato,
maraviglia non è se nudo e solo
resto prigion d'un cavalier armato.

Wherefore should I any longer vent
My keen wish in dour words and sighs
If by heaven, which gives the soul its guise,
No one late or early of this fate is rent.
Why on more pining is my tired heart bent
If others too must die? so for these eyes
The hours of my ending will be less wry
For there's no joy can match my torment.
So if the blow from him stolen and flown
I cannot dodge, if it's destined at best,
Who'll stand between the sweet and moan?
If beat and captured I must be blessed,
It is no wonder that naked and alone
Of an armed cavalier the captive I rest.

Perché Febo non torce e non distende
d'intorn' a questo globo freddo e molle
le braccia sua lucenti, el vulgo volle
notte chiamar quel sol che non comprende.

E tant'è debol, che s'alcun accende
un picciol torchio, in quella parte tolle
la vita dalla notte, e tant'è folle
che l'esca col fucil la squarcia e fende.

E s'egli è pur che qualche cosa sia,
cert'è figlia del sol e della terra;
ché l'un tien l'ombra, e l'altro sol la cria.

Ma sia che vuol, che pur chi la loda erra,
vedova, scura, in tanta gelosia,
c'una lucciola sol gli può far guerra.

Since Phoebus does not wind or split
All round this cold damp ball
His lucent arms, folk want to call
Night the sun beyond their wit.
Yet it's so weak that if one lit
The least torch there one may pall
The life of the night, so flimsy withal
A tinderbox rives and cleaves it.
And if indeed it did exist some bit,
Of sun and earth it is sure daughter,
One shadow bears, the other sires it.
Be what she may, who praises errs,
Widowed, dark and in such jealous fit
A single firefly can wage war on her.

O notte, o dolce tempo, benché nero,
con pace ogn' opra sempr' al fin assalta;
ben vede e ben intende chi t'esalta,
e chi t'onor' ha intelletto intero.
   Tu mozzi e tronchi ogni stanco pensiero
che l'umid' ombra e ogni quiet' appalta,
e dall'infima parte alla più alta
in sogno spesso porti ov'ire spero.
   O ombra del morir, per cui si ferma
ogni miseria a l'alma, al cor nemica,
ultimo delli afflitti e buon rimedio,
   tu rendi sana nostra carn' inferma,
rasciughi i pianti e posi ogni fatica,
e furi a chi ben vive ogn'ira e tedio.

O night, O sweet time, however black
With peace each task you at last assail;
Well they see you and well grasp who hail,
Sound mind your liegemen do not lack.
Each tired thought you clip away and hack
Who moist shade and every quiet bails,
To the heights I hope from the deep vale
In dream you often bear me back.
O shadow of death, whereby has end
All woe hostile to the soul, to the heart,
The afflicted's last and lasting remedy;
This infirm flesh of ours you mend,
You dry our tears and set all toil apart,
And lift off the living all rage and ennui.

Ogni van chiuso, ogni coperto loco,
quantunche ogni materia circumscrive,
serba la notte, quando il giorno vive,
contro al solar suo luminoso gioco.

E s'ella è vinta pur da fiamma o foco,
da lei dal sol son discacciate e prive
con più vil cosa ancor sue specie dive,
tal c'ogni verme assai ne rompe o poco.

Quel che resta scoperto al sol, che ferve
per mille vari semi e mille piante,
il fier bifolco con l'aratro assale;

      ma l'ombra sol a piantar l'uomo serve.
Dunche, le notti più ch'e' dì son sante,
quanto l'uom più d'ogni altro frutto vale.

Each shut room, each covered place the same,
That matter surrounds everywhichway,
Keeps safe the night in the living day,
Against its lightsome solar game.
Though she's beaten by fire or flame,
The sun deprives and drives away
Her divine looks – as viler things may,
Since a worm can more or less maim.
What lies uncovered to the sun, broiling
With a thousand seeds and verdure,
The proud peasant with his plough assays,
But only shadow serves man's sowing.
Thus night is than the day more pure
As all other fruit does man outweigh.

Colui che fece, e non di cosa alcuna,
il tempo, che non era anzi a nessuno,
ne fe' d'un due e diè 'l sol alto all'uno,
all'altro assai più presso diè la luna.

Onde 'l caso, la sorte e la fortuna
in un momento nacquer di ciascuno;
e a me consegnaro il tempo bruno,
come a simil nel parto e nella cuna.

E come quel che contrafà se stesso,
quando è ben notte, più buio esser suole,
ond'io di far ben mal m'affliggo e lagno.

Pur mi consola assai l'esser concesso
far giorno chiar mia oscura notte al sole
che a voi fu dato al nascer per compagno.

He who, and not out of anything, begot
Time, which before was not for anyone,
Made of one two, gave the far sun to one,
The moon to the other, nearer by a lot.
Hence, chance, fortune and fate's plot
Were born in an instant for everyone
And to me the dark time they passed on
As to one similar at birth and in the cot.
And as with one who himself to copy sets,
It's wont to get darker when night's well on,
So doing ill well I blame myself and mourn.
Yet it consoles me greatly that I'm now let
Make clear day my dark night in the sun
That was given you as companion when born.

Non vider gli occhi miei cosa mortale
allor che ne' bei vostri intera pace
trovai, ma dentro, ov'ogni mal dispiace,
chi d'amor l'alma a sé simil m'assale;
    e se creata a Dio non fusse equale,
altro che 'l bel di fuor, c'agli occhi piace,
più non vorria; ma perch'è si fallace,
trascende nella forma universale.
    Io dico c'a chi vive quel che muore
quetar non può disir; né par s'aspetti
l'eterno al tempo, ove altri cangia il pelo.
    Voglia sfrenata el senso è, non amore,
che l'alma uccide; e 'l nostro fa perfetti
gli amici qui, ma più per morte in cielo.

My eyes did not see a thing of mortal norm
When in your lovely ones whole ease
I found, but inside, where ill displeases,
He who my soul, like to Him, with loving storms;
And if created, to God it did not conform
It would only wants what the eye pleases,
Outside beauty; but since that with lies teases,
It goes beyond into the universal form.
I say that what dies, for those who live,
Cannot appease desire; nor does one expect
The eternal of time, where men grow hoar.
Unbridleness is the senses, not love, that give
Death to the soul; and ours makes perfect
Friends here, but by death in heaven more.

Per ritornar là donde venne fora,
l'immortal forma al tuo carcer terreno
venne com'angel di pietà sì pieno,
che sana ogn'intelletto e 'l mondo onora.

Questo sol m'arde e questo m'innamora,
non pur di fuora il tuo volto sereno:
c'amor non già di cosa che vien meno
tien ferma speme, in cui virtù dimora.

Né altro avvien di cose altere e nuove
in cui si preme la natura, e 'l cielo
è c'a' lor parti largo s'apparecchia;

né Dio, suo grazia, mi si mostra altrove
più che 'n alcun leggiadro e mortal velo;
e quel sol amo perch'in lui si specchia.

In its returning whence it had strayed
The immortal form to your earthly prison place
Came like an angel so lavish of solace
It heals all minds and the world's honour paid.
This alone fires me and my love's swayed
Not by the outward of your serene face
Since love in which dwells virtue's grace
Has never high hope of things that fade.
No different befalls things new and rare
Where nature strives, heaven does not fail
At their birthing to let its bounty brim;
Nor does God, in his mercy, show elsewhere
More than in a comely and a mortal veil
And that I love only that it mirrors him.

Gli occhi miei vaghi delle cose belle
e l'alma insieme della suo salute
non hanno altra virtute
c'ascenda al ciel, che mirar tutte quelle.
Dalle più alte stelle
discende uno splendore
che 'l desir tira a quelle,
e qui si chiama amore.
Né altro ha il gentil core
che l'innamori e arda, e che 'l consigli,
c'un volto che negli occhi lor somigli.

My eyes for fair things all afire
And my soul for its redemption
Have both no other option
For heaven than such things to admire.
From the stars set higher
Down pours a radiance clear
That to such draws desire,
And that is called love here.
Kind heart has naught else near
To beguile it, and kindle and to advise
Than a face that's like them in its eyes.

G 108

Indarno spera, come 'l vulgo dice,
chi fa quel che non de' grazia o mercede.
Non fui, com'io credetti, in voi felice,
privandomi di me per troppa fede,
né spero com'al sol nuova fenice
ritornar più; ché 'l tempo nol concede.
Pur godo il mie gran danno sol perch'io
son più mie vostro, che s'i' fussi mio.

G 108

In vain he hopes, says the vulgar crew,
In grace or mercy who does what is not fit.
I was not, as I'd thought, happy in you,
Denying me myself through too much credit,
Nor do I hope as in the sun a phoenix new
To turn again; for time does not allow it.
Yet I relish my hard hurt for this fact alone
I am more mine yours than if I were my own.

Non sempre a tutti è sì pregiato e caro
quel che 'l senso contenta,
c'un sol non sia che 'l senta,
se ben par dolce, pessimo e amaro.
Il buon gusto è sì raro
c'al vulgo errante cede
in vista, allor che dentro di sé gode.
Così, perdendo, imparo
quel che di fuor non vede
chi l'alma ha trista, e' suo sospir non ode.
El mondo è cieco e di suo gradi o lode
più giova a chi più scarso esser ne vuole,
come sferza che 'nsegna e parte duole.

Not always is so precious and dear to all
What the senses sates,
There be not one who rates,
Though seeming sweet, wretched as gall.
Good taste is so rare withal
That it stoops to the mistaken crew,
– would seem – for inward gladness lies.
So though I lose I yet recall,
What outwardly they see not who
Have mean souls and do not heed its sighs.
The world is blind, its praise and prize
More profit those who want least part
Like a lash that teaches while it smarts.

Non è senza periglio
il tuo volto divino
dell'alma a chi è vicino
com'io a morte, che la sento ognora;
ond'io m'armo e consiglio
per far da quel difesa anzi ch'i' mora.
Ma tuo mercede, ancora
che 'l fin sie da presso,
non mi rende a me stesso;
né danno alcun da tal pietà mi scioglie:
ché l'uso di molt'anni un dì non toglie.

It is not without peril
Your countenance divine
To the soul of one in line
As I for death, which each hour I know;
So I arm myself, take council
To ward myself from it before I go.
For your bounty, although
The end is now before,
Me to myself won't restore
Nor damnation of such pietà rid me;
Habit of years a day doesn't make free.

Sotto duo belle ciglia
le forze Amor ripiglia
nella stagion che sprezza l'arco e l'ale.
Gli occhi mie, ghiotti d'ogni maraviglia
c'a questa s'assomiglia,
di lor fan pruova a più d'un fero strale.
E parte pur m'assale,
appresso al dolce, un pensier aspro e forte
di vergogna e di morte;
né perde Amor per maggior tema o danni:
c'un'or non vince l'uso di molt'anni.

Under two lashes fair
Love its strength repairs
In an age that mocks the wings and the bow
My eyes, for all prodigy astare
That to this likeness bear,
Taste from them more than one fierce arrow.
And yet I feel the blow,
With the sweets before, of thoughts sharp and sour
Of shame and death's power;
But Love doesn't cede to greater harm or fears:
For an hour won't beat back the habit of years.

Sol perché tuo e bellezze al mondo sièno
eterne al tempo che le dona e fura,
prego se ne ripigli la natura
tutte quelle c'ognor ti vengon meno,
   e serbi a riformar del tuo sereno
e divin volto una gentil figura
del ciel, e sia d'amor perpetua cura
rifarne un cor di grazia e pietà pieno.
   E serbi poi i mie sospiri ancora,
e le lacrime sparte insieme accoglia
e doni a chi quella ami un'altra volta.
   Forse a pietà chi nascerà in quell'ora
lo moverà con la mie strema doglia,
né fie persa la grazia c'or m'è tolta.

Just that your great beauty in the world be
Eternal in time, which gives then steals the same,
I plead that nature now reclaim
All that which now fades from thee,
Keep it to reshape from your serenity
And godliness of face a noble frame,
Heavenly, that it be love's perpetual aim
To remake a heart full of grace and pity.
And may it keep my sighs still new,
And with them the shed tears cull so,
To the one who loves him give them back.
Whoever on that hour is born to rue
He'll move him with my fearful woe,
So the grace I'm now bereft of may not lack.

Ben può talor col mie 'rdente desio
salir la speme e non esser fallace,
ché s'ogni nostro affetto al ciel dispiace,
a che fin fatto arebbe il mondo Iddio?
    Qual più giusta cagion dell'amart'io
è, che dar gloria a quella eterna pace
onde pende il divin che di te piace,
e c'ogni cor gentil ha fatto casto e pio?
    Amor non è, signor mie, quell'amore
con la beltà, c'ogni momento scema,
ond'è suggetta al variar d'un bel viso.
    Dolce è ben quella in un pudico core,
che per cangiar di scorza o d'ora strema
non manca, e qui caparra il paradiso.

Well can my deep desire at times not sole
Rise up with my hope nor be a lying tease,
For if all our fondness heaven displease,
Wherefore would God have made the whole?
For my loving you what more proper goal
Is there than glorifying that eternal ease
Whence hangs the divine in you does please,
And makes chaste and pious each gentle soul?
Love is not that love, lord of mine,
For beauty, which does every moment wane,
Hence change in a fair face must undergo.
Sweet indeed is that, in a heart that's fine,
Which in outer change or our last pain
Fades not, and pledges paradise below.

Non è sempre di colpa aspra e mortale
d'una immensa bellezza un fero ardore,
se poi sì lascia liquefatto il core,
ch 'n breve il penetri un divino strale.

Amore isveglia e desta e 'mpenna l'ale,
né l'alto vol preschive al van furore;
qual primo grado c'al suo creatore,
di quel non sazia, l'alma ascende e sale.

L'amor di quel ch'i parlo in alto aspira;
donna è dissimil troppo; e mal conviensi
arder di quella al cor saggio e verile.

L'un tira al cielo, e l'altro in terra tira;
nell'alma l'un, l'altr'abita ne' sensi,
e l'arco tira a cose basse e vile.

Not always is a bitter and mortal hit
For immense beauty an ardent pride,
Should it leave the soul all liquefied
So an arrow divine may easy pierce it.
Love does rouse and stir, with wings outfit,
Nor from high soaring vain passion chide;
This the first step, for with that not satisfied,
Soul ascends and climbs to who created it.
The love of which I speak aspires the height;
Woman's too different far; and it fits not well
The wise and virile heart for her to be aglow.
One at heaven aims, downward the other's sight;
One in the soul, in sense does the other dwell,
Bending the bow at things vile and low.

Notes

G. 56. Advisory: i.t.o. l. 3: 'anguish and death'. Licence for such small beer will not be asked again. Michelangelo drafted his poems on scraps of paper, on the back or in the margin of letters he had received and on the back of sketches and drawings. Although this has helped resolve some problems of dating, it has also created others. This quatrain appears on the back of a letter from Sebastiano del Piombo dated 8 June 1532. Michelangelo did not come again to Rome, after a first visit in 1496, until the September of 1532. One of his first great editors, Karl Frey (1897), believes, however, that the quatrain was composed for de'Cavalieri. If so, it is the first of the sequence.

G. 57. l. 1: *cuoce*, cooks. It is unlikely that the reference is to the kitchen, rather to the process of mortar- or paint-making.

G. 58. ll. 3, 4: i.t.o. 'perhaps still in the house of Love/it would make pitiful who pitiless rules'. I have inverted ll. 5 and 6; *legge*, law.

G. 59. l. 1: *uphold*: imported for the rhyme; ll. 7 and 8 rearranged with some inversion.

G. 60. l. 2: *goderti più da presso*, 'enjoy you from nearer to'. l. 6: *che m'è concesso*, 'which is granted me'.

G. 61. ll. 2, 3: *sole . . . suole*, the rhyme indicates not only the habitual nature of the phoenix's rearising but, through '*suolo*': soil, links sky and earth. For semantic reasons I have had to reposition *ond'io tutt'ardo*, hence missing a second meaning: old age, 'whence I am all on fire'.

G. 62. l. 4: the end of l. 6 and the beginning of l. 7 have changed places.

G. 63. l. 4: the image is that of mortar binding stones into a building. I have inverted ll. 7 and 8 and dropped *al ciel*, 'to heaven'.

G. 64. Various translators give 'dovecot' for *covon*. I can find no linguistic reason for this, though in Tuscany and elsewhere I have seen dovecots of straw.

G. 65. l. 4: i.t.o. 'where I dwell'.

G. 72. The end of l. 5 and the beginning of l. 6 have changed places. I.t.o. l. 13: 'my desired sweet lord'.

G. 74. Apart from failing to resolve these lines without accenting a past participle, I have had to change the word order slightly.

G. 75. l. 1: *intorno*, around; l. 4: *'bright'*, imported; l. 6: *canti*, 'songs, tunes'.

G. 76. l. 7: *un non so*, 'un je-ne-sais-quoi'.

G. 77. I have changed the order of phrases in ll. 6 and 7. It may be that *la visiva virtù* means the power of seeing, but the causal *per* suggests it is a quality of the object of sight.

G. 78. l. 5: i.t.o. 'there where truth is mute'. There are various, but obvious, changes to the order of phrases in the second quatrain.

G. 79. l. 13: *turpissime*. Though this might translate as 'disgraceful', such would imply that Michelangelo thought there was a morally reprehensible element, rather than something to be deprecated out of artistic modesty, in the drawings sent to Cavalieri, drawings that were his own 'fair copy' of subjects sketched by the pupil and on which the latter had invited the master's correction. Both Frey and Girardi suggest that what Michelangelo received in return were writings that revitalized people. Ettore Barelli reads *persone* as singular. It is possible that that the plural was elicited by the need to rhyme with *scrive*. See the preamble to these notes.

G. 80. l. 3: rhyme has caused me to blind the eagle rather than merely close, or fix, its eyes. It is certainly possible to read l. 8 to mean that the intellect is also vainly cast away if it would match God.

G. 81. A madrigal. I have shifted *somiglia*, 'resembles', l. 9, to my following line.

G. 82. l. 2: i.t.o. 'earthly remains'; l. 6: 'deprives and strips me'. The second quatrain contains various ambiguities. *Amor* could be the subject of *pensar*, *minuir*, and *viene*, as could *morte*. Less probable readings: 'as a result of thinking to diminish the pain you caused me by imitating you, Love comes to give me death'; 'my pain, thinking to diminish itself by doubling, comes to give me death'; and others.

G. 83. I.t.o. l. 6: 'marks and points out'. My *true grown* is *onesto* in l. 8 of the

original; *quel pietoso fonte*, l. 9, I have expanded for the sake of rhyme. By chang-
ing the order of phrases in the first terzina I have also have excluded a possible
meaning: 'all beauty which those aware see more than anything else here'.

G. 84. I.t.o. l. 4: 'what our talent can draw forth'; l. 6: 'all humble endeavour'.

G. 87. It is on the basis of the handwriting that Girardi attributes this sonnet
to the Cavalieri period. I.t.o. l. 11: 'the world'. The bride in l. 13 is more likely
to be the soul than the Catholic Church.

G. 88. l. 4: My rhyme requires balance for 'weight'. Translators have taken
inteso, l. 5, to mean 'understood', whereas it seems to have the philosophical
nuance of intentionality: 'sole object of my mind'.

G. 90. I.t.o. l. 2: 'I am worth more than myself'; l. 9: 'Safe with this mark in
every place/I go'. All the rhymes of the octet are in ...*oglio* or ...*aglio*. The
Cavalier's balladeer could hardly have made things more difficult for himself.

G. 92. Madrigal. l. 4: *pellegrine*, 'far wandering'. l. 10: 'most doubtful of the
quiet life beyond'.

G. 93. Madrigal. Published with the music of Jacques Arcadelt, master of the
Sistine Choir, in his *Primo libro de madrigali a quattro voce* (1539–40), perhaps
the most famous book of madrigals ever composed. I had to shift *senso* nearer
to its verb in l. 3.

G. 94. The *vil bruto* is a silkworm. Whatever the *pianelle* of l. 12 are, they are
not, as winter wear, slippers, but, given the *colonna* of the previous line, they
are more likely pattens. I have taken licence for *bootikins* from the general tone
of amused sexual fantasy.

G. 95. l. 8: *visivo acume*, 'power (or acuteness) of sight'.

G. 96. Three tercets, probably from a longer composition.

G. 97. I could not catch the octet's front rhyme in *al*. In ll. 5 and 6, *zoppa*
governs *al vischio, a' lacci*.

G. 98. One of the two sonnets in the Cavalieri cycle (the other is G. 101
following) in which the sestet rhymes CDCDCD. The words 'lights' – the *luci*
of l. 7 – is still used in English for 'eyes'. The last line puns on Cavalieri's name.

G. 101. One of several poems lamenting the death of Febo del Poggio, another young man Michelangelo loved in the early period of his attachment to Cavalieri. Frey believes this sonnet, and the three that follow, to have been written at the time of the painting of *The Last Judgement* and sent to Cavalieri. I could not find rhymes to keep apart the octet and the sestet. For this, and for the other three 'night' sonnets following, Girardi has more recently (1991) suggested the date of c.1545.

G. 102. I have chosen to see in l. 7 a Dantean reference, hence *vale* for the undifferentiated *parte*, and a reference to G. 83. Having had to shorten and shift *ov'ire spero* from l. 8, I have lost the nuances of 'whither . . .' or 'hence I hope to go'.

G. 103. I.t.o. l. 1: 'Every shut room, every covered place'. l. 4: *ogni verme*: 'We are all worms,' Churchill is supposed to have said, 'but some of us are glowworms.' See G. 101.

G. 105. I.t.o. l. 1: 'mortal thing'. I have changed the order of phrases in ll. 5 and 6.

G. 106. I.t.o. l. 1: 'whence it emerged'.

G. 107. Madrigal. I could find no rhyme that would bind together the objects to be viewed or seen in ll. 1, 4, 5, 7 as they are bound in the original.

G. 108. Autonomous octet. I.t.o. l. 7: 'my great harm'.

G. 109. Madrigal. l. 12: *più scarso esser ne vuole* might also mean 'whom it [the world] least wants to benefit from them'.

G. 130. Madrigal. I have used *pietà* in l. 10 because the feeling referred to may well be what Michelangelo feels for Cavalieri, in parallel to *tuo mercede*.

G. 131. l. 4: Eyes can be bigger than bellies: *ghiotti*, 'greedy, over-fond'.

G. 230. I have taken the text of an earlier version addressed to a man.

G. 259. l. 9 is taken from an earlier version.

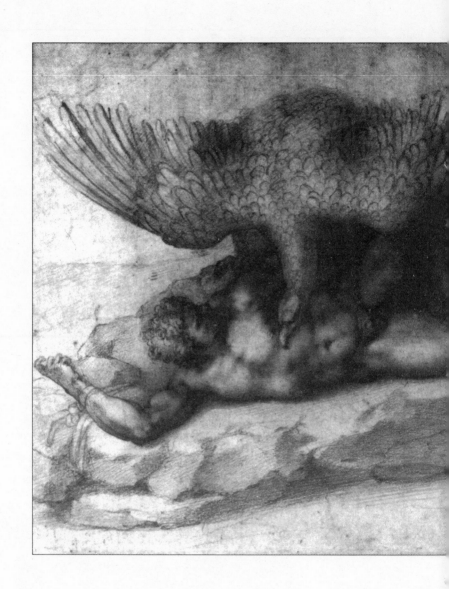